# THE
# DANGEROUS
# GAME

# THE MOST DANGEROUS GAME

*by*
Richard Connell

W
*Wisehouse Classics*

Richard Connell

*The Most Dangerous Game*

Published by Wisehouse Classics – Sweden

ISBN 978-91-7637-879-3

Wisehouse Classics is a Wisehouse Imprint.

© Wisehouse 2020 – Sweden

www.wisehouse-publishing.com

"Off there to the right—somewhere—is a large island," said Whitney. "It's rather a mystery—"

"What island is it?" Rainsford asked.

"The old charts call it 'Ship-Trap Island,'" Whitney replied. "A suggestive name, isn't it? Sailors have a curious dread of the place. I don't know why. Some superstition—"

"Can't see it," remarked Rainsford, trying to peer through the dank tropical night that was palpable as it pressed its thick warm blackness in upon the yacht.

"You've good eyes," said Whitney, with a laugh, "and I've seen you pick off a moose moving in the brown fall bush at four hundred yards, but even you can't see four miles or so through a moonless Caribbean night."

"Nor four yards," admitted Rainsford. "Ugh! It's like moist black velvet."

"It will be light enough in Rio," promised Whitney. "We should make it in a few days. I hope the jaguar guns have come from Purdey's. We should have some good hunting up the Amazon. Great sport, hunting."

"The best sport in the world," agreed Rainsford.

"For the hunter," amended Whitney. "Not for the jaguar."

"Don't talk rot, Whitney," said Rainsford. "You're a big-game hunter, not a philosopher. Who cares how a jaguar feels?"

"Perhaps the jaguar does," observed Whitney.

"Bah! They've no understanding."

"Even so, I rather think they understand one thing—fear. The fear of pain and the fear of death."

"Nonsense," laughed Rainsford. "This hot weather is making you soft, Whitney. Be a realist. The world is made up of two classes—the hunters and the huntees. Luckily, you and I are hunters. Do you think we've passed that island yet?"

"I can't tell in the dark. I hope so."

"Why?" asked Rainsford.

"The place has a reputation—a bad one."

"Cannibals?" suggested Rainsford.

"Hardly. Even cannibals wouldn't live in such a God-forsaken place. But it's gotten into sailor lore, somehow. Didn't you notice that the crew's nerves seemed a bit jumpy today?"

"They were a bit strange, now you mention it. Even Captain Nielsen—"

"Yes, even that tough-minded old Swede, who'd go up to the devil himself and ask him for a light. Those fishy blue eyes held a look I never saw there before. All I could get out of him was 'This place has an evil name among seafaring men, sir.' Then he said to me, very gravely, 'Don't you feel anything?'—as if the air about us was actually poisonous. Now, you mustn't laugh when I tell you this—I did feel something like a sudden chill.

"There was no breeze. The sea was as flat as a plate-glass window. We were drawing near the island then. What I felt was a—a mental chill; a sort of sudden dread."

"Pure imagination," said Rainsford.

"One superstitious sailor can taint the whole ship's company with his fear."

"Maybe. But sometimes I think sailors have an extra sense that tells them when they are in danger. Sometimes I think evil is a tangible thing—with wave lengths, just as sound and light have. An evil place can, so to speak, broadcast vibrations of evil. Anyhow, I'm glad we're getting out of this zone. Well, I think I'll turn in now, Rainsford."

"I'm not sleepy," said Rainsford. "I'm going to smoke another pipe up on the afterdeck."

"Good night, then, Rainsford. See you at breakfast."

"Right. Good night, Whitney."

There was no sound in the night as Rainsford sat there but the muffled throb of the engine that drove the yacht swiftly through the darkness, and the swish and ripple of the wash of the propeller.

Rainsford, reclining in a steamer chair, indolently puffed on his favorite brier. The sensuous drowsiness of the night was on him. "It's so dark," he thought, "that I could sleep without closing my eyes; the night would be my eyelids—"

An abrupt sound startled him. Off to the right he heard it, and his ears, expert in such matters, could not be mistaken. Again he heard the sound, and again. Somewhere, off in the blackness, someone had fired a gun three times.

Rainsford sprang up and moved quickly to the rail, mystified. He strained his eyes in the direction from which the reports had come, but it was like trying to see through a blanket. He leaped upon the rail and balanced himself there, to get greater elevation; his pipe, striking a rope, was knocked from his mouth. He lunged for it; a short, hoarse cry came from his lips as he realized he had reached too far and had lost his balance. The cry was pinched off short as the blood-warm waters of the Caribbean Sea closed over his head.

He struggled up to the surface and tried to cry out, but the wash from the speeding yacht slapped him in the face and the salt water in his open mouth made him gag and strangle. Desperately he struck out with strong strokes after the receding lights of the yacht, but he stopped before he had swum fifty feet. A certain coolheadedness had come to him; it was not the first time he had been in a tight place. There was a chance that his cries could be heard by someone aboard the yacht, but that chance was slender and grew more slender as the yacht raced on. He wrestled himself out of his clothes and shouted with all his power. The lights of the yacht became faint and ever-vanishing fireflies; then they were blotted out entirely by the night.

Rainsford remembered the shots. They had come from the right, and doggedly he swam in that direction, swimming with slow, deliberate strokes, conserving his strength. For a seemingly endless time he fought the sea. He began to count his strokes; he could do possibly a hundred more and then—

Rainsford heard a sound. It came out of the darkness, a high screaming sound, the sound of an animal in an extremity of anguish and terror.

He did not recognize the animal that made the sound; he did not try to; with fresh vitality he swam toward the sound. He heard it again; then it was cut short by another noise, crisp, staccato.

"Pistol shot," muttered Rainsford, swimming on.

Ten minutes of determined effort brought another sound to his ears— the most welcome he had ever heard—the muttering and growling of the sea breaking on a rocky shore. He was almost on the rocks before he saw them; on a night less calm he would have been shattered against them. With his remaining strength he dragged himself from the swirling waters. Jagged crags appeared to jut up into the opaqueness; he forced himself upward, hand over hand. Gasping, his hands raw, he reached a flat place at the top. Dense jungle came down to the very edge of the cliffs. What perils that tangle of trees and underbrush might hold for him did not concern Rainsford just then. All he knew was that he was safe from his enemy, the sea, and that utter weariness was on him. He flung himself down at the jungle edge and tumbled headlong into the deepest sleep of his life.

When he opened his eyes he knew from the position of the sun that it was late in the afternoon. Sleep had given him new vigor; a sharp hunger was picking at him. He looked about him, almost cheerfully.

"Where there are pistol shots, there are men. Where there are men, there is food," he thought. But what kind of men, he wondered, in so forbidding a place? An unbroken front of snarled and ragged jungle fringed the shore.

He saw no sign of a trail through the closely knit web of weeds and trees; it was easier to go along the shore, and Rainsford floundered along by the water. Not far from where he landed, he stopped.

Some wounded thing—by the evidence, a large animal—had thrashed about in the underbrush; the jungle weeds were crushed down and the moss was lacerated; one patch of weeds was stained crimson. A small, glittering object not far away caught Rainsford's eye and he picked it up. It was an empty cartridge.

"A twenty-two," he remarked. "That's odd. It must have been a fairly large animal too. The hunter had his nerve with him to tackle it with a light gun. It's clear that the brute put up a fight. I suppose the first three shots I heard was when the hunter flushed his quarry and wounded it. The last shot was when he trailed it here and finished it."

He examined the ground closely and found what he had hoped to find—the print of hunting boots. They pointed along the cliff in the direction he had been going. Eagerly he hurried along, now slipping on a rotten log or a loose stone, but making headway; night was beginning to settle down on the island.

Bleak darkness was blacking out the sea and jungle when Rainsford sighted the lights. He came upon them as he turned a crook in the coast line; and his first thought was that be had come upon a village, for there were many lights. But as he forged along he saw to his great astonishment that all the lights were in one enormous building—a lofty structure with pointed towers plunging upward into the gloom. His eyes made out the shadowy outlines of a palatial chateau; it was set on a high bluff, and on three sides of it cliffs dived down to where the sea licked greedy lips in the shadows.

"Mirage," thought Rainsford. But it was no mirage, he found, when he opened the tall spiked iron gate. The stone steps were real enough;

the massive door with a leering gargoyle for a knocker was real enough; yet above it all hung an air of unreality.

He lifted the knocker, and it creaked up stiffly, as if it had never before been used. He let it fall, and it startled him with its booming loudness. He thought he heard steps within; the door remained closed. Again Rainsford lifted the heavy knocker, and let it fall. The door opened then—opened as suddenly as if it were on a spring—and Rainsford stood blinking in the river of glaring gold light that poured out. The first thing Rainsford's eyes discerned was the largest man Rainsford had ever seen—a gigantic creature, solidly made and black bearded to the waist. In his hand the man held a long-barreled revolver, and he was pointing it straight at Rainsford's heart.

Out of the snarl of beard two small eyes regarded Rainsford.

"Don't be alarmed," said Rainsford, with a smile which he hoped was disarming. "I'm no robber. I fell off a yacht. My name is Sanger Rainsford of New York City."

The menacing look in the eyes did not change. The revolver pointing as rigidly as if the giant were a statue. He gave no sign that he understood Rainsford's words, or that he had even heard them. He was dressed in uniform—a black uniform trimmed with gray astrakhan.

"I'm Sanger Rainsford of New York," Rainsford began again. "I fell off a yacht. I am hungry."

The man's only answer was to raise with his thumb the hammer of his revolver. Then Rainsford saw the man's free hand go to his forehead in a military salute, and he saw him click his heels together and stand at attention. Another man was coming down the broad marble steps, an erect, slender man in evening clothes. He advanced to Rainsford and held out his hand.

In a cultivated voice marked by a slight accent that gave it added precision and deliberateness, he said, "It is a very great pleasure and honor to welcome Mr. Sanger Rainsford, the celebrated hunter, to my home."

Automatically Rainsford shook the man's hand.

"I've read your book about hunting snow leopards in Tibet, you see," explained the man. "I am General Zaroff."

Rainsford's first impression was that the man was singularly handsome; his second was that there was an original, almost bizarre quality about the general's face. He was a tall man past middle age, for his hair was a vivid white; but his thick eyebrows and pointed military mustache were as black as the night from which Rainsford had come. His eyes, too, were black and very bright. He had high cheekbones, a sharpcut nose, a spare, dark face—the face of a man used to giving orders, the face of an aristocrat. Turning to the giant in uniform, the general made a sign. The giant put away his pistol, saluted, withdrew.

"Ivan is an incredibly strong fellow," remarked the general, "but he has the misfortune to be deaf and dumb. A simple fellow, but, I'm afraid, like all his race, a bit of a savage."

"Is he Russian?"

"He is a Cossack," said the general, and his smile showed red lips and pointed teeth. "So am I."

"Come," he said, "we shouldn't be chatting here. We can talk later. Now you want clothes, food, rest. You shall have them. This is a mostrestful spot."

Ivan had reappeared, and the general spoke to him with lips that moved but gave forth no sound.

"Follow Ivan, if you please, Mr. Rainsford," said the general. "I was about to have my dinner when you came. I'll wait for you. You'll find that my clothes will fit you, I think."

It was to a huge, beam-ceilinged bedroom with a canopied bed big enough for six men that Rainsford followed the silent giant. Ivan laid out an evening suit, and Rainsford, as he put it on, noticed that it came from a London tailor who ordinarily cut and sewed for none below the rank of duke.

The dining room to which Ivan conducted him was in many ways remarkable. There was a medieval magnificence about it; it suggested a baronial hall of feudal times with its oaken panels, its high ceiling, its vast refectory tables where twoscore men could sit down to eat. About the hall were mounted heads of many animals—lions, tigers, elephants, moose, bears; larger or more perfect specimens Rainsford had never seen. At the great table the general was sitting, alone.

"You'll have a cocktail, Mr. Rainsford," he suggested. The cocktail was surpassingly good; and, Rainsford noted, the table appointments were of the finest—the linen, the crystal, the silver, the china.

They were eating *borsch*, the rich, red soup with whipped cream so dear to Russian palates. Half apologetically General Zaroff said, "We do our best to preserve the amenities of civilization here. Please forgive any lapses. We are well off the beaten track, you know. Do you think the champagne has suffered from its long ocean trip?"

"Not in the least," declared Rainsford. He was finding the general a most thoughtful and affable host, a true cosmopolite. But there was one small trait of the general's that made Rainsford uncomfortable. Whenever he looked up from his plate he found the general studying him, appraising him narrowly.

"Perhaps," said General Zaroff, "you were surprised that I recognized your name. You see, I read all books on hunting published in English, French, and Russian. I have but one passion in my life, Mr. Rainsford, and it is the hunt."

"You have some wonderful heads here," said Rainsford as he ate a particularly well-cooked *filet mignon*. "That Cape buffalo is the largest I ever saw."

"Oh, that fellow. Yes, he was a monster."

"Did he charge you?"

"Hurled me against a tree," said the general. "Fractured my skull. But I got the brute."

"I've always thought," said Rainsford, "that the Cape buffalo is the most dangerous of all big game."

For a moment the general did not reply; he was smiling his curious red-lipped smile. Then he said slowly, "No. You are wrong, sir. The Cape buffalo is not the most dangerous big game." He sipped his wine. "Here in my preserve on this island," he said in the same slow tone, "I hunt more dangerous game."

Rainsford expressed his surprise. "Is there big game on this island?"

The general nodded. "The biggest."

"Really?"

"Oh, it isn't here naturally, of course. I have to stock the island."

"What have you imported, general?" Rainsford asked. "Tigers?"

The general smiled. "No," he said. "Hunting tigers ceased to interest me some years ago. I exhausted their possibilities, you see. No thrill left in tigers, no real danger. I live for danger, Mr. Rainsford."

The general took from his pocket a gold cigarette case and offered his guest a long black cigarette with a silver tip; it was perfumed and gave off a smell like incense.

"We will have some capital hunting, you and I," said the general. "I shall be most glad to have your society."

"But what game—" began Rainsford.

"I'll tell you," said the general. "You will be amused, I know. I think I may say, in all modesty, that I have done a rare thing. I have invented a new sensation. May I pour you another glass of port?"

"Thank you, general."

The general filled both glasses, and said, "God makes some men poets. Some He makes kings, some beggars. Me He made a hunter. My hand was made for the trigger, my father said. He was a very rich man with a quarter of a million acres in the Crimea, and he was an ardent sportsman. When I was only five years old he gave me a little gun, specially made in Moscow for me, to shoot sparrows with. When I shot some of his prize turkeys with it, he did not punish me; he complimented me on my marksmanship. I killed my first bear in the Caucasus when I was ten. My whole life has been one prolonged hunt. I went into the army—it was expected of noblemen's sons—and for a time commanded a division of Cossack cavalry, but my real interest was always the hunt. I have hunted every kind of game in every land. It would be impossible for me to tell you how many animals I have killed."

The general puffed at his cigarette.

"After the debacle in Russia I left the country, for it was imprudent for an officer of the Czar to stay there. Many noble Russians lost everything. I, luckily, had invested heavily in American securities, so I shall never have to open a tearoom in Monte Carlo or drive a taxi in Paris. Naturally, I continued to hunt—grizzlies in your Rockies, crocodiles in the Ganges, rhinoceroses in East Africa. It was in Africa that the Cape buffalo hit me and laid me up for six months. As soon as I recovered I started for the Amazon to hunt jaguars, for I had heard they were unusually cunning. They weren't." The Cossack sighed. "They were no match at all for a hunter with his wits about him, and a high-powered rifle. I was bitterly disappointed. I was lying in my tent with a splitting headache one night when a terrible thought pushed its way into my mind. Hunting was beginning to bore me! And hunting, remember, had been my life. I have heard that in America businessmen often go to pieces when they give up the business that has been their life."

"Yes, that's so," said Rainsford.

The general smiled. "I had no wish to go to pieces," he said. "I must do something. Now, mine is an analytical mind, Mr. Rainsford. Doubtless that is why I enjoy the problems of the chase."

"No doubt, General Zaroff."

"So," continued the general, "I asked myself why the hunt no longer fascinated me. You are much younger than I am, Mr. Rainsford, and have not hunted as much, but you perhaps can guess the answer."

"What was it?"

"Simply this: hunting had ceased to be what you call `a sporting proposition.' It had become too easy. I always got my quarry. Always. There is no greater bore than perfection."

The general lit a fresh cigarette.

"No animal had a chance with me any more. That is no boast; it is a mathematical certainty. The animal had nothing but his legs and his instinct. Instinct is no match for reason. When I thought of this it was a tragic moment for me, I can tell you."

Rainsford leaned across the table, absorbed in what his host was saying.

"It came to me as an inspiration what I must do," the general went on.

"And that was?"

The general smiled the quiet smile of one who has faced an obstacle and surmounted it with success. "I had to invent a new animal to hunt," he said.

"A new animal? You're joking." "Not at all," said the general. "I never joke about hunting. I needed a new animal. I found one. So I bought this island, built this house, and here I do my hunting. The island is perfect for my purposes—there are jungles with a maze of traits in them, hills, swamps—"

"But the animal, General Zaroff?"

"Oh," said the general, "it supplies me with the most exciting hunting in the world. No other hunting compares with it for an instant. Every day I hunt, and I never grow bored now, for I have a quarry with which I can match my wits."

Rainsford's bewilderment showed in his face.

"I wanted the ideal animal to hunt," explained the general. "So I said, `What are the attributes of an ideal quarry?' And the answer was, of course, 'It must have courage, cunning, and, above all, it must be able to reason.'"

"But no animal can reason," objected Rainsford.

"My dear fellow," said the general, "there is one that can."

"But you can't mean—" gasped Rainsford.

"And why not?"

"I can't believe you are serious, General Zaroff. This is a grisly joke."

"Why should I not be serious? I am speaking of hunting."

"Hunting? Great Guns, General Zaroff, what you speak of is murder."

The general laughed with entire good nature. He regarded Rainsford quizzically. "I refuse to believe that so modern and civilized a young man as you seem to be harbors romantic ideas about the value of human life. Surely your experiences in the war—"

"Did not make me condone cold-blooded murder," finished Rainsford stiffly.

Laughter shook the general. "How extraordinarily droll you are!" he said. "One does not expect nowadays to find a young man of the educated class, even in America, with such a naive, and, if I may say so, mid-Victorian point of view. It's like finding a snuffbox in a limousine. Ah, well, doubtless you had Puritan ancestors. So many Americans appear to have had. I'll wager you'll forget your notions when you go hunting with me. You've a genuine new thrill in store for you, Mr. Rainsford."

"Thank you, I'm a hunter, not a murderer."

"Dear me," said the general, quite unruffled, "again that unpleasant word. But I think I can show you that your scruples are quite ill founded."

"Yes?"

"Life is for the strong, to be lived by the strong, and, if needs be, taken by the strong. The weak of the world were put here to give the strong pleasure. I am strong. Why should I not use my gift? If I wish to hunt, why should I not? I hunt the scum of the earth: sailors from tramp ships—lascars, blacks, Chinese, whites, mongrels—a thoroughbred horse or hound is worth more than a score of them."

"But they are men," said Rainsford hotly.

"Precisely," said the general. "That is why I use them. It gives me pleasure. They can reason, after a fashion. So they are dangerous."

"But where do you get them?"

The general's left eyelid fluttered down in a wink. "This island is called Ship Trap," he answered. "Sometimes an angry god of the high seas sends them to me. Sometimes, when Providence is not so kind, I help Providence a bit. Come to the window with me."

Rainsford went to the window and looked out toward the sea.

"Watch! Out there!" exclaimed the general, pointing into the night. Rainsford's eyes saw only blackness, and then, as the general pressed a button, far out to sea Rainsford saw the flash of lights.

The general chuckled. "They indicate a channel," he said, "where there's none; giant rocks with razor edges crouch like a sea monster with wide-open jaws. They can crush a ship as easily as I crush this nut." He dropped a walnut on the hardwood floor and brought his heel grinding down on it. "Oh, yes," he said, casually, as if in answer to a question, "I have electricity. We try to be civilized here."

"Civilized? And you shoot down men?"

A trace of anger was in the general's black eyes, but it was there for but a second; and he said, in his most pleasant manner, "Dear me, what a righteous young man you are! I assure you I do not do the thing you suggest. That would be barbarous. I treat these visitors with every consideration. They get plenty of good food and exercise. They get into splendid physical condition. You shall see for yourself tomorrow."

"What do you mean?"

"We'll visit my training school," smiled the general. "It's in the cellar. I have about a dozen pupils down there now. They're from the Spanish bark *San Lucar* that had the bad luck to go on the rocks out there. A very inferior lot, I regret to say. Poor specimens and more accustomed to the deck than to the jungle." He raised his hand, and Ivan, who served as waiter, brought thick Turkish coffee. Rainsford, with an effort, held his tongue in check.

"It's a game, you see," pursued the general blandly. "I suggest to one of them that we go hunting. I give him a supply of food and an excellent hunting knife. I give him three hours' start. I am to follow, armed only with a pistol of the smallest caliber and range. If my quarry eludes me for three whole days, he wins the game. If I find him"—the general smiled—"he loses."

"Suppose he refuses to be hunted?"

"Oh," said the general, "I give him his option, of course. He need not play that game if he doesn't wish to. If he does not wish to hunt, I turn him over to Ivan. Ivan once had the honor of serving as official knouter to the Great White Czar, and he has his own ideas of sport. Invariably, Mr. Rainsford, invariably they choose the hunt."

"And if they win?"

The smile on the general's face widened. "To date I have not lost," he said. Then he added, hastily: "I don't wish you to think me a braggart, Mr. Rainsford. Many of them afford only the most elementary sort of problem. Occasionally I strike a tartar. One almost did win. I eventually had to use the dogs."

"The dogs?"

"This way, please. I'll show you."

The general steered Rainsford to a window. The lights from the windows sent a flickering illumination that made grotesque patterns on the courtyard below, and Rainsford could see moving about there a dozen or so huge black shapes; as they turned toward him, their eyes glittered greenly.

"A rather good lot, I think," observed the general. "They are let out at seven every night. If anyone should try to get into my house—or out of it—something extremely regrettable would occur to him." He hummed a snatch of song from the *Folies Bergere.*

"And now," said the general, "I want to show you my new collection of heads. Will you come with me to the library?"

"I hope," said Rainsford, "that you will excuse me tonight, General Zaroff. I'm really not feeling well."

"Ah, indeed?" the general inquired solicitously. "Well, I suppose that's only natural, after your long swim. You need a good, restful night's sleep. Tomorrow you'll feel like a new man, I'll wager. Then we'll hunt, eh? I've one rather promising prospect—" Rainsford was hurrying from the room.

"Sorry you can't go with me tonight," called the general. "I expect rather fair sport—a big, strong, black. He looks resourceful—Well, good night, Mr. Rainsford; I hope you have a good night's rest."

The bed was good, and the pajamas of the softest silk, and he was tired in every fiber of his being, but nevertheless Rainsford could not quiet his brain with the opiate of sleep. He lay, eyes wide open. Once he thought he heard stealthy steps in the corridor outside his room. He sought to throw open the door; it would not open. He went to the window and looked out. His room was high up in one of the towers. The lights of the chateau were out now, and it was dark and silent; but there was a fragment of sallow moon, and by its wan light he could see, dimly, the courtyard. There, weaving in and out in the pattern of shadow, were black, noiseless forms; the hounds heard him at the window and looked up, expectantly, with their green eyes. Rainsford went back to the bed and lay down. By many methods he tried to put himself to sleep. He had achieved a doze when, just as morning began to come, he heard, far off in the jungle, the faint report of a pistol.

General Zaroff did not appear until luncheon. He was dressed faultlessly in the tweeds of a country squire. He was solicitous about the state of Rainsford's health.

"As for me," sighed the general, "I do not feel so well. I am worried, Mr. Rainsford. Last night I detected traces of my old complaint."

To Rainsford's questioning glance the general said, "Ennui. Boredom."

Then, taking a second helping of *crêpes Suzette*, the general explained: "The hunting was not good last night. The fellow lost his head. He made a straight trail that offered no problems at all. That's the trouble with these sailors; they have dull brains to begin with, and they do not know how to get about in the woods. They do excessively stupid and obvious things. It's most annoying. Will you have another glass of *Chablis*, Mr. Rainsford?"

"General," said Rainsford firmly, "I wish to leave this island at once."

The general raised his thickets of eyebrows; he seemed hurt. "But, my dear fellow," the general protested, "you've only just come. You've had no hunting—"

"I wish to go today," said Rainsford. He saw the dead black eyes of the general on him, studying him. General Zaroff's face suddenly brightened.

He filled Rainsford's glass with venerable *Chablis* from a dusty bottle.

"Tonight," said the general, "we will hunt—you and I."

Rainsford shook his head. "No, general," he said. "I will not hunt."

The general shrugged his shoulders and delicately ate a hothouse grape. "As you wish, my friend," he said. "The choice rests entirely with you. But may I not venture to suggest that you will find my idea of sport more diverting than Ivan's?"

He nodded toward the corner to where the giant stood, scowling, his thick arms crossed on his hogshead of chest.

"You don't mean—" cried Rainsford.

"My dear fellow," said the general, "have I not told you I always mean what I say about hunting? This is really an inspiration. I drink to a foeman worthy of my steel—at last." The general raised his glass, but Rainsford sat staring at him.

"You'll find this game worth playing," the general said enthusiastically. "Your brain against mine. Your woodcraft against mine. Your strength and stamina against mine. Outdoor chess! And the stake is not without value, eh?"

"And if I win—" began Rainsford huskily.

"I'll cheerfully acknowledge myself defeat if I do not find you by midnight of the third day," said General Zaroff. "My sloop will place you on the mainland near a town." The general read what Rainsford was thinking.

"Oh, you can trust me," said the Cossack. "I will give you my word as a gentleman and a sportsman. Of course you, in turn, must agree to say nothing of your visit here."

"I'll agree to nothing of the kind," said Rainsford.

"Oh," said the general, "in that case—But why discuss that now? Three days hence we can discuss it over a bottle of *Veuve Cliquot*, unless—"

The general sipped his wine.

Then a businesslike air animated him. "Ivan," he said to Rainsford, "will supply you with hunting clothes, food, a knife. I suggest you wear moccasins; they leave a poorer trail. I suggest, too, that you avoid the big swamp in the southeast corner of the island. We call it Death Swamp. There's quicksand there. One foolish fellow tried it. The deplorable part of it was that Lazarus followed him. You can imagine my feelings, Mr. Rainsford. I loved Lazarus; he was the finest hound in my pack. Well, I must beg you to excuse me now. I always take a siesta after lunch. You'll hardly have time for a nap, I fear. You'll want to start, no doubt. I shall not follow till dusk. Hunting at night is so much more exciting than by day, don't you think? Au revoir, Mr. Rainsford, au revoir." General Zaroff, with a deep, courtly bow, strolled from the room.

From another door came Ivan. Under one arm he carried khaki hunting clothes, a haversack of food, a leather sheath containing a long-bladed hunting knife; his right hand rested on a cocked revolver thrust in the crimson sash about his waist.

Rainsford had fought his way through the bush for two hours. "I must keep my nerve. I must keep my nerve," he said through tight teeth.

He had not been entirely clearheaded when the chateau gates snapped shut behind him. His whole idea at first was to put distance between himself and General Zaroff; and, to this end, he had plunged along, spurred on by the sharp rowers of something very like panic. Now he had got a grip on himself, had stopped, and was taking stock of himself and the situation. He saw that straight flight was futile; inevitably it would bring him face to face with the sea. He was in a picture with a frame of water, and his operations, clearly, must take place within that frame.

"I'll give him a trail to follow," muttered Rainsford, and he struck off from the rude path he had been following into the trackless wilderness. He executed a series of intricate loops; he doubled on his trail again and again, recalling all the lore of the fox hunt, and all the dodges of the fox. Night found him leg-weary, with hands and face lashed by the branches, on a thickly wooded ridge. He knew it would be insane to blunder on through the dark, even if he had the strength. His need for rest was imperative and he thought, "I have played the fox, now I must play the cat of the fable." A big tree with a thick trunk and outspread branches was near by, and, taking care to leave not the slightest mark, he climbed up into the crotch, and, stretching out on one of the broad limbs, after a fashion, rested. Rest brought him new confidence and almost a feeling of security. Even so zealous a hunter as General Zaroff could not trace him there, he told himself; only the devil himself could follow that complicated trail through the jungle after dark. But perhaps the general was a devil—

An apprehensive night crawled slowly by like a wounded snake and sleep did not visit Rainsford, although the silence of a dead world was on the jungle. Toward morning when a dingy gray was varnishing the sky, the cry of some startled bird focused Rainsford's attention in that direction. Something was coming through the bush, coming slowly, carefully, coming by the same winding way Rainsford had come. He flattened himself down on the limb and, through a screen of leaves almost as thick as tapestry, he watched… . That which was approaching was a man.

It was General Zaroff. He made his way along with his eyes fixed in utmost concentration on the ground before him. He paused, almost beneath the tree, dropped to his knees and studied the ground. Rainsford's impulse was to hurl himself down like a panther, but he saw that the general's right hand held something metallic—a small automatic pistol.

The hunter shook his head several times, as if he were puzzled. Then he straightened up and took from his case one of his black cigarettes; its pungent incenselike smoke floated up to Rainsford's nostrils.

Rainsford held his breath. The general's eyes had left the ground and were traveling inch by inch up the tree. Rainsford froze there, every muscle tensed for a spring. But the sharp eyes of the hunter stopped before they reached the limb where Rainsford lay; a smile spread over his brown face. Very deliberately he blew a smoke ring into the air; then he turned his back on the tree and walked carelessly away, back along the trail he had come. The swish of the underbrush against his hunting boots grew fainter and fainter.

The pent-up air burst hotly from Rainsford's lungs. His first thought made him feel sick and numb. The general could follow a trail through the woods at night; he could follow an extremely difficult trail; he must have uncanny powers; only by the merest chance had the Cossack failed to see his quarry.

Rainsford's second thought was even more terrible. It sent a shudder of cold horror through his whole being. Why had the general smiled? Why had he turned back?

Rainsford did not want to believe what his reason told him was true, but the truth was as evident as the sun that had by now pushed through the morning mists. The general was playing with him! The general was saving him for another day's sport! The Cossack was the cat; he was the mouse. Then it was that Rainsford knew the full meaning of terror.

"I will not lose my nerve. I will not."

He slid down from the tree, and struck off again into the woods. His face was set and he forced the machinery of his mind to function. Three hundred yards from his hiding place he stopped where a huge dead tree leaned precariously on a smaller, living one. Throwing off his sack of food, Rainsford took his knife from its sheath and began to work with all his energy.

The job was finished at last, and he threw himself down behind a fallen log a hundred feet away. He did not have to wait long. The cat was coming again to play with the mouse.

Following the trail with the sureness of a bloodhound came General Zaroff. Nothing escaped those searching black eyes, no crushed blade of grass, no bent twig, no mark, no matter how faint, in the moss. So intent was the Cossack on his stalking that he was upon the thing Rainsford had made before he saw it. His foot touched the protruding bough that was the trigger. Even as he touched it, the general sensed his danger and leaped back with the agility of an ape. But he was not quite quick enough; the dead tree, delicately adjusted to rest on the cut living one, crashed down and struck the general a glancing blow on the shoulder as it fell; but for his alertness, he must have been smashed beneath it. He staggered, but he did not fall; nor did he drop his revolver. He stood there, rubbing his injured shoulder, and Rainsford, with fear again gripping his heart, heard the general's mocking laugh ring through the jungle.

"Rainsford," called the general, "if you are within sound of my voice, as I suppose you are, let me congratulate you. Not many men know how to make a Malay mancatcher. Luckily for me I, too, have hunted in Malacca. You are proving interesting, Mr. Rainsford. I am going now to have my wound dressed; it's only a slight one. But I shall be back. I shall be back."

When the general, nursing his bruised shoulder, had gone, Rainsford took up his flight again. It was flight now, a desperate, hopeless flight, that carried him on for some hours. Dusk came, then darkness, and still he pressed on. The ground grew softer under his moccasins; the vegetation grew ranker, denser; insects bit him savagely.

Then, as he stepped forward, his foot sank into the ooze. He tried to wrench it back, but the muck sucked viciously at his foot as if it were a giant leech. With a violent effort, he tore his feet loose. He knew where he was now. Death Swamp and its quicksand.

His hands were tight closed as if his nerve were something tangible that someone in the darkness was trying to tear from his grip. The softness of the earth had given him an idea. He stepped back from the quicksand a dozen feet or so and, like some huge prehistoric beaver, he began to dig.

Rainsford had dug himself in in France when a second's delay meant death. That had been a placid pastime compared to his digging now. The pit grew deeper; when it was above his shoulders, he climbed out and from some hard saplings cut stakes and sharpened them to a fine point. These stakes he planted in the bottom of the pit with the points sticking up. With flying fingers he wove a rough carpet of weeds and branches and with it he covered the mouth of the pit. Then, wet with sweat and aching with tiredness, he crouched behind the stump of a lightning-charred tree.

He knew his pursuer was coming; he heard the padding sound of feet on the soft earth, and the night breeze brought him the perfume of the general's cigarette. It seemed to Rainsford that the general was coming with unusual swiftness; he was not feeling his way along, foot by foot.

Rainsford, crouching there, could not see the general, nor could he see the pit. He lived a year in a minute. Then he felt an impulse to cry aloud with joy, for he heard the sharp crackle of the breaking branches as the cover of the pit gave way; he heard the sharp scream of pain as the pointed stakes found their mark. He leaped up from his place of concealment. Then he cowered back. Three feet from the pit a man was standing, with an electric torch in his hand.

"You've done well, Rainsford," the voice of the general called. "Your Burmese tiger pit has claimed one of my best dogs. Again you score. I think, Mr. Rainsford, I'll see what you can do against my whole pack. I'm going home for a rest now. Thank you for a most amusing evening."

At daybreak Rainsford, lying near the swamp, was awakened by a sound that made him know that he had new things to learn about fear. It was a distant sound, faint and wavering, but he knew it. It was the baying of a pack of hounds.

Rainsford knew he could do one of two things. He could stay where he was and wait. That was suicide. He could flee. That was postponing the inevitable. For a moment he stood there, thinking. An idea that held a wild chance came to him, and, tightening his belt, he headed away from the swamp.

The baying of the hounds drew nearer, then still nearer, nearer, ever nearer. On a ridge Rainsford climbed a tree. Down a watercourse, not a quarter of a mile away, he could see the bush moving. Straining his eyes, he saw the lean figure of General Zaroff; just ahead of him Rainsford made out another figure whose wide shoulders surged through the tall jungle weeds; it was the giant Ivan, and he seemed pulled forward by some unseen force; Rainsford knew that Ivan must be holding the pack in leash.

They would be on him any minute now. His mind worked frantically. He thought of a native trick he had learned in Uganda. He slid down the tree. He caught hold of a springy young sapling and to it he fastened his hunting knife, with the blade pointing down the trail; with a bit of wild grapevine he tied back the sapling. Then he ran for his life. The hounds raised their voices as they hit the fresh scent. Rainsford knew now how an animal at bay feels.

He had to stop to get his breath. The baying of the hounds stopped abruptly, and Rainsford's heart stopped too. They must have reached the knife.

He shinned excitedly up a tree and looked back. His pursuers had stopped. But the hope that was in Rainsford's brain when he climbed died, for he saw in the shallow valley that General Zaroff was still on his feet. But Ivan was not. The knife, driven by the recoil of the springing tree, had not wholly failed.

Rainsford had hardly tumbled to the ground when the pack took up the cry again.

"Nerve, nerve, nerve!" he panted, as he dashed along. A blue gap showed between the trees dead ahead. Ever nearer drew the hounds. Rainsford forced himself on toward that gap. He reached it. It was the shore of the sea. Across a cove he could see the gloomy gray stone of the chateau. Twenty feet below him the sea rumbled and hissed. Rainsford hesitated. He heard the hounds. Then he leaped far out into the sea…

When the general and his pack reached the place by the sea, the Cossack stopped. For some minutes he stood regarding the blue-green expanse of water. He shrugged his shoulders. Then be sat down, took a drink of brandy from a silver flask, lit a cigarette, and hummed a bit from *Madame Butterfly*.

General Zaroff had an exceedingly good dinner in his great paneled dining hall that evening. With it he had a bottle of *Pol Roger* and half a bottle of *Chambertin*. Two slight annoyances kept him from perfect enjoyment. One was the thought that it would be difficult to replace Ivan; the other was that his quarry had escaped him; of course, the American hadn't played the game—so thought the general as he tasted his after-dinner liqueur. In his library he read, to soothe himself, from the works of Marcus Aurelius. At ten he went up to his bedroom. He was deliciously tired, he said to himself, as he locked himself in. There was a little moonlight, so, before turning on his light, he went to the window and looked down at the courtyard. He could see the great hounds, and he called, "Better luck another time," to them. Then he switched on the light.

A man, who had been hiding in the curtains of the bed, was standing there.

"Rainsford!" screamed the general. "How in God's name did you get here?"

"Swam," said Rainsford. "I found it quicker than walking through the jungle."

The general sucked in his breath and smiled. "I congratulate you," he said. "You have won the game."

Rainsford did not smile. "I am still a beast at bay," he said, in a low, hoarse voice. "Get ready, General Zaroff."

The general made one of his deepest bows. "I see," he said. "Splendid! One of us is to furnish a repast for the hounds. The other will sleep in this very excellent bed. On guard, Rainsford... "

He had never slept in a better bed, Rainsford decided.

37490815R00019

dressing room full of costumes, identities, and pathways to greatness. For example, Thomas Edison became unsatisfied with darkness, so he invented a way to create his own light.

When you put darkness into a healthy perspective, you realize it opens the gateway to innovation. Dark areas in life are opportunities, doorways from which many of us run fearfully rather than pass through.

> *Dark areas in life are actually opportunities, doorways from which many run fearfully rather than pass through.*

History teaches us the pinnacle of life's most beautiful and coveted creations come from tough pathways. Think about diamonds which come from the dark and dusty coalmine, magnificent landscapes such as mountains, valleys, and islands that come out of earthquakes, tsunamis, and hurricanes. In short, what we categorized as devastation and destruction, God sees as sculpting and preparation.

Just as many successful achievers say it is impossible to have success without many failures, it is these failures and rejections and shortcomings that birth success and achievements.

Remember... it cannot be faith if you can already see the outcome. It's a thin line between faith and belief, and you need both. Faith is trusting, and belief is fully depending on that trust.

## FAITH vs. BELIEF

However, on another note, the path of the unknown is one taken by the elite and kings of the world. This is a good time to talk about a familiar question—a comparison of the difference between *faith* and *belief.*

Faith is "a mental blueprint of thoughts, arranged to form an outcome, energized by emotions and supportive beliefs." To make this as simple as A+B+C, if you are building a tree swing, faith would be the idea that says, "If I take a rope and throw it over a tree branch, then tie it to a flat piece of wood, I will be able to swing on it..."

Faith, by appearance, is looking forward, whether toward the next moment or the next day or week. It's also trust... trust in a person, place, or thing, just as when you sit on a chair and expect it will hold your weight. We also witness faith when someone allows another to carry the weight of a problem, circumstance, or issue for them. If someone threatens you and you call the police, you pass the problem to another resource better equipped to handle it, entrusting them because of your faith.

*Faith is also trust... just as when you sit on a chair and expect it will hold your weight.*

Proverbs 3:5-6 records a clear definition of how faith works. To paraphrase, it coaches us to trust in God and not depend on our own wisdom, education, or past experiences. In every encounter we should recognize that God is in control and He will give direction.

Biblical faith is the material that builds and nurtures all dreams and desires—whether it's a car, fame, money, or health. Faith and trust in God can get it done. Why is that such a big thing? Because God is the creator and He likes when we appreciate who He is. This is why He hates pride. Even a prideful look. It's like us when we work hard at something but someone else takes credit.

*Biblical faith is the material that builds and nurtures dreams.*

God is a Father, and He wants nothing but to take care of His children. Faith from a human perspective appears unfair. However, it's a gift from God to those who recognize him as the ultimate Father of creation.

In Job 13:15, Job says, "Even though he slays me, yet I will trust him." As a father of six reading that scripture, I think of how it is sometimes necessary to discipline my children, verbally or physically. Shortly after the tears and emotional flood, they still have no doubt of my love, as well as my protection.

True faith says, I know God created everything and everyone, and understands how things operate, as well as how people operate. Who better to turn over control to?

When we lose control, without big trouble and terror-inducing situations, we think we don't need faith. Faith is usually reserved for events beyond our control.

Now belief is something your mind holds as a guarantee. When you show up for work and clock in, you believe because of that clock punch that you will be paid for the day. You experience no uncertainty at all.

People use the word "faith" all the time, but when they hear it in sermons they become confused, because what they've read and experienced about faith appear very different.

In all my studies about a champion's mindset, they substitute a different word for faith—the *unknown*. This term is used by the alpha business and world leaders who operate in the unknown, shaking their Bibles and dancing. They are changing the world, building cultures, empires, and changing lives, which God intended His people to do.

Don't get me wrong. I am very much a Christian. I take the Bible seriously and this is why I had to write this book. But remember faith, through God's own words, has the power to move mountains, raise the dead, and cause change. Faith says it's going to work itself out; we don't know

*Belief does not accept "no" as an option.*

how, but it will, even though we can't touch it, taste it, nor see it. We simply trust with all our might.

Belief does not say anything. It's simply over and done. Belief does not accept *no* as an option. It does not question how Jesus was able to live a life without compromise, in spite of all the scorn, gossip, insults, and challenges, without retaliating or quitting. Jesus believed in his purpose, his goal, his desire—to save our lives from depression, anxiety, hurt, harm, and danger, and to bring us into a life of fulfillment, accomplishment, and abundance, as noted in John 10:10. It was Jesus' passion to bring people to wholeness. God in the flesh. What other need can you think of? Like the old saying goes, what do you give a man who has everything? The answer is the love of his loved ones.

## The Action of AMEN

I absolutely love when I fully understand a word or phrase. I believe that knowledge, when used for its original purpose, is the real power.

For most of the world, the word "amen" is the period at the end of a prayer. However, God never wastes any words. He is extremely detailed, therefore every word has a purpose and is placed on purpose.

In relationship to faith and belief, I bring your attention to *amen*, which is defined as "so be it" or "it is so." This complements the whole action of belief as well as faith. It is spoken at the conclusion of a request made in prayer. It is spoken out of trust and belief that the prayer request will happen. The emotions of joy and happiness await the manifestation.

*Amen* can also be a seal of forever and always. In the book of Deuteronomy, we see its use in a negative form, as a salutation of a curse to an adulteress and covenant breakers, making their curses a life sentence.

Amen is mentioned in other Old Testament verses. One is a request of God being praised forever and for his glory to be present always. In the final book of the Bible, Revelation 3:14, Jesus is mentioned as "the amen," the beginning of Creation, faithful and true. In Revelation 1:17, Jesus tells us he is the first and the last, also known as always and forever.

My point here is when you're facing tough times, when life is strangling you and you are forced to pray, if you don't pray automatically, put iron in your faith and belief—say "amen" with confidence. Put the seal of forever and always in your request, and as we learned here, become your request.

If you're praying for freedom from oppression, come out of your prayer with the emotions that support your freedom. If you're praying for financial security, come out of your prayer with the emotions, expectations, and confidence of financial security. This is why God always stated to come to Him with boldness, because we have the power to ask and receive if only we have faith and believe.

## The On/Off Switch

This book is intended as an adrenaline shot, so let me inform you that you possess a mental switch, just like an on/off switch, that can actually turn on the light as well as the darkness of life.

We control that switch via the beliefs we hold dear. Whether it's a desired belief or an unwanted belief caused by a past or current situation, at our very foundation, we control whatever we accept.

At one time or another we have been told that nobody can make us do anything we would not ultimately choose to do. There are no witches, warlocks, or mutants with superhuman powers who can make you physically do anything. You yourself have to consciously decide what you will do.

We tell ourselves that we allow a situation to determine our choice, but we make the decision. We have the power, so why not use that power toward what we want? Toward the desires that makes us happy, successful, and powerful?

*You have the power to decide to be in a good mood.*

I understand if it sounds easy but appears impossible. Imagine if you were in a bad mood, but someone you know and trust tells you good news. Your mental state changes dramatically. A simple truth is that the good news did not eliminate whatever had put you in a bad mood. But it shifted your focus to the mood you preferred, which was a good mood.

Most disturbing is that there are a few people who refuse to be happy, often due to an emotional trauma that was brought on by a potential happy moment.

This book is a redbull read intended to begin the healing process in the eye of a crisis, so whenever an opportunity to transition from a bad mood to a good mood is present, I want you to know the choice is ultimately up to you.

I'm a huge fight sports fan and the best moments are when both fighters are tired, worn out, hurting, and mentally exhausted. The coaches in the corners are screaming, "Dig deep," meaning persist, push yourself to the chosen goal. When drama arises and the negativity is weighing down on you, dig deep. Hit that mental switch to turn on the light. You don't have to live in the dark, no matter the situation.

Getting upset is a learned response. It's a habit we picked up from our upbringing. Living in the streets is considered rock bottom in the United States, but in many foreign countries, whole communities of people live in mud huts, or homes consisting only of recycled metal or even sticks. They are content, without mental breakdowns.

Choice comes from within. Within is your *spirit*. It is the everlasting You, the You that never dies. It will do what's in your own best interest. Turn it on. Choose light, and happiness, peace, and comfort.

## Believe in the Dark

This is a simple idea. When tough and confusing times occur, have an encouraging belief that better days are coming. There is no reason to go catatonic or confine yourself in a mental prison.

Often you do not have all the answers. When you don't know what to do, many wise and educated people have suggested you should press forward, continuing motion, showing that the circumstance doesn't rule you; *you* rule you. This makes a path for life to provide a desired outcome, freeing your emotions and concentration to hear, see, and find that outcome without distractions that mute and blind you.

> *To believe in the dark means that when all hope seems lost, you still believe in your own survival.*

To believe in the dark means that when all hope seems lost, you still believe in your own survival. Instill within yourself a dream, a positive outcome, a reason to move on despite the situations and motions that add pressure.

The inspirational speaking culture calls it "your why." Your why is an unconditional inspiration that continues on auto-pilot, even when you want to quit. The most important part of this process is the belief.

It's time for you to take a bold step. Believing is seeing. What you focus on, you adapt to. Pattern your life to complement that perception.

In tough times and through periods of consistent change, you will know that adjustments are coming. Instead of crumbling and falling into anxiety or depression due to lack of control, you will hold fast to your belief.

Having a proper understanding of belief and applying it to your mental resources through repetition gives you the ability to *see in the dark!*

# 3
# The Artform of Getting Through

Now that we've defined "belief" and "dark," it's time to put the two together, allowing your belief to help see you through dark times. This is an artform you will perfect over time. I purposely use the term *artform,* because as in every art, its application takes discipline, technique, and practice.

With the full understanding of true belief, knowing how to operate in it, and apply the proper perspective to the unknown, you have begun your study into this important craft. Next is to build the habit and discipline, through repetition, to apply this helpful perspective in all circumstances.

The majority of crippling mental conditions come from not having concrete knowledge of what lies ahead. With proper time management, you can get some control of your mental steering wheel. I mean literally, minute by minute, hour by hour—or for extreme cases, second by second.

As funny as it sounds, if you learn to focus your attention seriously on what you will do, think, and feel, in the next thirty minutes you will be surprised at the emotional ease you develop.

*The majority of crippling mental conditions come from not having concrete knowledge of what lies ahead.*

When we worry, most of the devastating outcomes we predict never happen. We might waste days, weeks, or months mired in anxiety over the possibility of receiving an eviction notice, a terrible medical diagnosis, or of getting fired. Never mind the horror movies we simply dream up.

Dividing time properly within ourselves takes off the bulk of the pressure. The Bible teaches a pattern of thinking for everyday success. In Philippians, the apostle Paul says that whatever is true, honorable, right, pure, lovely, commendable, and brings excellence and praise should govern, rule, and be the template of your thinking.

You must personally take control of your thoughts and not allow anyone else to dictate your emotions or actions. This will be a dance with time, from awake to sleep. You must take the lead, because it's been proven that throughout the course of the day, the events that affect your subconscious get buried inside, creating a thought pattern that becomes your habitual mindset.

Paul also speaks about beating your body into submission so your thoughts come into your complete control. No, it's not an easy job, almost like catching a single mouse from among a group of mice. With little clarity, you will need to sort through all the available thoughts and responses, choosing healthy thoughts versus unhealthy thoughts, beneficial thoughts versus currently not helpful thoughts.

As an example, if you're in need of a mechanic, but focus on going to the gym, even though the latter thought is still healthy, it does not serve your best interests. Time management will help you understand the best thoughts and actions to help you achieve your long-term dreams and desire, and the appropriate time in which to undertake them.

## GET FAMILIAR

It's without dispute that when your mind and thoughts are healthy, everything else falls into place. The human capability, when harnessed properly, can create miracles. Remember those genius inventions and physical impossibilities?

When you talk about getting your mind healthy, meditation and other spiritual practices are always mentioned. So what is meditation? It is a way of getting familiar, through long and close association, through friendship or intimacy with yourself and your own thoughts.

If one desires to overcome a traumatic episode and chooses to meditate on it, true meditation says to spend time and build a relationship with the healing process. Get familiar with the object that heals what is damaged.

Say the trauma was a violent encounter with a random person. The damage is the mental reoccurrence of the situation. The healing happens through making sense of the reason behind the crisis, then ultimately allowing the event to pass out of everyday thought.

The meditation process familiarizes the meditator with the suggestion of the how and why of life's uncertainties. It suggests methods of resolution such as forgiveness and empathy. It then familiarizes the meditator with a life that exists after minimizing the effects of that memory. Becoming familiar with this more desirable life allows an attraction to that brighter future. The meditator can release all their energy and attention to the memory of that future feeling rather than the painful past occurrence.

*Healing happens through making sense of the reason behind the crisis.*

Meditation begins with relaxing the mind, commonly through breathing exercises, which medically decreases stress. The practice is done in a quiet place, with eyes closed and the concentration focused on the breath—not unlike the beginning of prayer.

When operating in daily life, especially in the midst of a crisis, I suggest the technique of "Stop, Drop and Pray." Use this reflex to build mental repetition.

If you look at Jesus as the ultimate example, he always halted his actions to speak to his Father in prayer. He secluded himself in preparation. When you pause to gather your thoughts, whether it's through prayer, meditation, or even to release emotions through tears or physical activity, familiarize yourself with your desired outcome. Stay consistent. As troubles and confusion come, grow an iron will. Be intimate and in a close friendship with your mental goals. Healing will be the eventual outcome.

*Prayer should become an everyday practice, not just a momentary response to crisis.*

Prayer should become an everyday practice, not just a momentary response to crisis.

## 24/7

Think about the mental preparation to begin an average day. It starts during sleep. Your subconscious mind controls the bulk of your thinking. There are few things you can, for sure, claim to have total control of, let alone for which you can predict or control the outcome.

Regardless of nationality, or political, financial or religious status, we are all given the same twenty-four hours, seven days per week. Time is given to everyone.

Many will challenge this notion because of the habitual allowance of control we give to outside sources and people in governance. Look no further than the foundation of the mentally challenged and those who are titled "criminals." The commonality is that they make choices to do, say, think, and act however they choose. For the mentally challenged, it's a natural response; they are operating off the instinct that God himself gave every human to live free, not bound by fear or controlled by others' fear. For the criminal mind, the choice is to go to war for what's desired, challenging any obstacle that stands between them and their happiness.

What does this have to do with time in the twenty-four-hour day? The answer is *choice*. Each day we wake up to a new twenty-four-hour cycle. What we do within that cycle is entirely up to us. Everyone controls their choices. But what generally happens is that we are persuaded by other people, our circumstances, and our fears to make un-wanted decisions.

Here is a cheat sheet for future healthier days. Look at what times you generally sleep, add your work hours, your play hours, then look within yourself to discover when you are your taking action toward your goals and dreams. Does this complement the life you most desire?

| | |
|---|---|
| 1_____ | 13 _____ |
| 2_____ | 14 _____ |
| 3_____ | 15 _____ |
| 4 _____ | 16 _____ |
| 5_____ | 17_____ |
| 6 _____ | 18 _____ |
| 7_____ | 19 _____ |
| 8 _____ | 20 _____ |
| 9 _____ | 21 _____ |
| 10 _____ | 22 _____ |
| 11 _____ | 23 _____ |
| 12 _____ | 24 _____ |

Life is a kaleidoscope of moments. They happen by seconds, minutes, and even days. Do not let anyone or anything steal your moments!

Take careful inventory of your moments. This is the first step to living a life of purpose... a life on purpose.

The biggest issue you face with time is how you approach it. Time is continuous and has no attachments.

We have trouble graduating to the next stage because we are holding on to the past, expecting past scenarios to repeat, negatively influencing our emotions, future events, and outcomes. When you cling so tightly to what happened in the past, you simply can't move forward. It's an anchor that keeps weighing you in the same place.

If you allow eight out of every twenty-four hours for sleep, that still leaves you sixteen more in which to create new situations, or contain or release an emotion, or even create a new perspective or personality. Yes, you can establish a fresh identity! What I'm saying is that when you spend time with yourself—looking at your loves, hates, objects of excitement, and so on—a lot can happen in as little as ten minutes!

Literally speaking, I want you to take your time. What I mean is I want you to stop your mental processing and cut everyone and everything else off. Instead, spend some time understanding yourself. Once you have that understanding, use it as a foundation to build yourself, your life, and your world from there.

I say it again; this is a quick-fix read to help you find that fresh start to a new life you've been craving.

Take charge of your time daily, hourly, minute by minute. As God has spoken, all things are possible.

A fair warning: Many of your family, friends, and co-workers will likely take issue with your new norm. However, please allow that to be *their issue*. Do not take this problem inside your own mental routine.

*When you take charge of your time, family and friends may take issue with this. Please allow that to be their issue, not yours.*

It's a common thought amongst Christians that, when we die, we will stand before the Lord God Almighty and give an account of our life, an account of what we did with our God-given purpose, talents, and gifts. Remember that this life is your time. More importantly, it's your life to develop.

It will take patience—a word most people in a crisis don't want to hear. That's because we commonly misunderstand the power of patience, especially when it comes to personal change. Instead we agonize over negative worries, allowing ourselves to not take action. Why not do and enjoy the opposite? Use the power of faith, belief, and meditation to discern and manifest the goals you truly want, patiently constructing them in your real life.

## The Story of Patience

The story of *patience* is usually portrayed in a negative light, as something to be tolerated. Often it's equated with its cousin, *waiting*. Waiting means to stop, be still, and do nothing. However, patience is a persistent motion while awaiting an outcome. You don't stop your progress toward a destination, you merely continue to build toward that stronger outcome.

> *Patience is not the same thing as waiting.*

Patience is its own kind of faith. It trusts that keeping hope while waiting will be beneficial. The story of patience is an action movie, not a fairy tale or a suspenseful drama.

Like God after creating the world, he rested, stopping to observe what had been done. The faith of patience allows us to know that progress can still be made even when we're not actively doing, or even awake. Sleep is a huge sign of faith. Know that you can stop for rest.

When you're anxious, depressed, frustrated, or even angry, sleep deprivation is often both the reason and the result. Allow yourself to heal through faithful, hopeful patience, trusting the assignment to another, while taking comfort that all will work in your favor while you rest.

# Conclusion

To truly believe in the dark as a means to get through crisis, you must understand the outcome of your desire. Use every hour of the day, maintaining focus on that desire. Have a true knowledge of belief and marry it to your emotions. When the unforeseen happens, remember that crisis is just a dark place. You will be able to use your on/off switch to respond in a more powerful way once you have taken control over your time and faith.

Any fitness expert will tell you that consistency, persistence, and repetition are key. Whatever you want, think, and act upon daily, these things attract more of the same into your life.

Take a look at your daily mental intake. Compare that with your habitual attitude. Certainly you will see a match.

Going forward, have faith in the love that God has for you. God did not create people to be tortured their whole lives. There's a silver lining in the dark cloud; Jesus came with the message that God already loves you and has knowledge of your troubles.

The weak can become strong, the poor can become rich. How, you ask? Belief, which begins with faith—a faith conditioned in and through the unknown and unforeseen. Faith allows you to live in absolute mental freedom, the freedom brought on by persistence toward the goal of getting through.

Darkness—the hard times—must happen, just as day turns into night. Difficulties and challenges will naturally arise. However, you must greet those times with the proper perspective and response.

We were designed for love, joy, and peace. Like the fish out of water, we were not designed to handle anxiety, depression, or loneliness. This is why so many crumble when they hit a dark path in life. They don't know how to adapt.

*Darkness—the hard times— must happen, just as day turns into night.*

I'm speaking to you right now. You are supposed to be happy, fulfilled, and at peace. You are within reach of everything your heart desires. That is the gospel truth.

If you are reading this, then you are a survivor. And you will continue to survive! Fear not. Panic not. You've gone through adversity before, and next time you will be better prepared, with the knowledge that faith, belief, and momentum will carry you through, with discipline in this artform that allows you fresh perspective on life and the dark moments.

You've survived and gone to victories afterward. This journey we call life is not impossible, nor is it unfamiliar. You are already an expert in adversity, therefore you can dictate your future response when it comes to crisis. Whenever darkness occurs along your path, face it, address it, and accept the fight. Nothing just goes away until it's addressed and assigned a fate.

You may not understand the situation, or even know why it has chosen you, but fear not! Let your faith help you move forward in this artform of getting through crisis. Believe in the dark!

# About the Author

D. M. HOUSE is a native Marylander, grass roots Baltimorean, a solo parental artist of six amazing children, and a devoted friend of God who possesses six years of college study in Psychology, Counseling, and Biblical History.

He is dedicated to marketing simplified Truth to encourage harmony and understanding in society, providing clear understanding to life's transparency within the complex smoke and mirrors of distraction.

Made in the USA
Middletown, DE
28 August 2023

37490164R00033